Truths & Disguises

Some time last year I '   ɔt-
very-famous poet. Who   ɔly
wouldn't name her eve   ɪnt
thing is, she was criticising wɪɪɪɪ.ɪɪ ɪ   led
purely to formulaic banality. Whilst no longer a regular, ɪ m a
frequent participant at three of my local writers' groups, at
which I have come across some banality, certainly, but also the
whole spectrum from the excellent to the positively Vogon.
What attracts me to these gatherings even more than the
quality of the better work, though, is the sheer pleasure of
spending time with a bunch of people who care about poetry.

Half of the poets in this volume are people I met at writers'
groups (though one assures me that we'd met before, and why
should I doubt him?). And the others? Well, one I met when
we were both reading at an event in York. Another was giving
me a lift to work when we both 'came out' as writers. Another
was a friend-of-a-friend, who I guess I first thought of as a
songwriter. And the last I introduced to the joys of Middle
English literature as part of my 'day job'. A diverse bunch of
writers, encountered in diverse circumstances, but all sharing
that same love of poetry and all committed to developing their
own poetic voices.

So when, following the positive responses to my own
collection, *The Kind Ghosts* (ideal gift for all your friends and
family), Anthony at *bluechrome* asked if I'd like to pull together a
collection of new poets that I'd stumbled across here and there,
I didn't have to think too long about who to include: these
eight writers whose work had really impressed me by 'word of
mouth'. Their poems, I think, speak for themselves. But what
of the writers? Some have slept on my sofa; one danced to
Elvis with me in the small hours; one played with me in a very
loud rock band; a few have read with me in all sorts of places;
one invited me to exhibition openings; another came to mine;
a couple looked after me when I was very unwell. In short, a
sound bunch of people. Some have become dear friends, the

rest respected acquaintances with whom, most importantly, I have been able to share a heartfelt belief that poetry matters. And it's really exciting to be able to introduce you to their work.

I would like to thank Cherie Federico of *Aesthetica*, Adrian Tellwright of *Dream Catcher* and Jo Dodd of Worm Holes Books, York, for their workshops, readings and other events at which I first came into contact with half a dozen of the writers herein. This collection is dedicated to them and to everyone who, in whatever way, creates environments for the conversation about poetry.

Truth can come in many disguises. You'll find it in these pages.

Oz Hardwick
York, July 2005

Truths & Disguises

Published by bluechrome publishing 2005

2 4 6 8 10 9 7 5 3

First published in Great Britain in 2005 by
bluechrome publishing
PO Box 109,
Portishead, Bristol. BS20 7ZJ

www.bluechrome.co.uk

A CIP catalogue record for this book is available from the
British Library

ISBN   1-904781-77-2

Cover photograph © Oz Hardwick

Truths & Disguises

Contents

Amina Alyal

Amina Alyal

At the age of eight Amina Alyal caught herself writing a poem. Since then she has regularly sneaked off to do it again when she isn't looking. Her attitude to writing is nomadic – or perhaps goat-like – each poem is a leap towards a fresh perspective, a gaze (or graze) on a different landscape. She writes in a variety of fields, and poetry is just one of the things that results.

Gothic Black and White

Grey outside
and a second greyness seeps
over interiors, cobweb, brocade,
tortoiseshell patterns of gold and decay.
And, not quite tangibly, she hovers, Mother
        Madeleine,
having chosen the veil, amongst veils of a different
        order.
Once she reached down, and I touched her flesh;
flesh was all there under the plentiful cloth.
Then she was gone, away down another long hall.

The nun of Monza, close in her bricked-up cell,
might have seen visions,
but none of the kind that she wanted.

The Date

The iron, like the big sleek nose of an aeroplane,
zooms over diminutive cloth. It seems
all ready for the journey, and you
look at the clock, and blood surges
as you see how close it is to take-off.

Earlier, you ironed your hair.
Plucked eyebrows, filed nails,
sandpapered legs, folded notes
very small into a tiny purse.
All this straitening and flattening,
when you mean to billow out, fly out,
take a chance, take a leap:
you know this is what you were waiting for.

You have gazed through the bars of a cage
a shadows enclosing a fierce lovely beast
you were never quite able to see;

now the gates have been thrown wide open
and you can get as close as you like.

Moments

You and I
walk side by side.
Our long shadows go out
like Etruscan shades
to the rim of the world.

You and I
walk each side of a street, when
glaring with light
a hot stinking beast roars between us.

It leaves a gap,
warm like the bed of a bear.

My grandfather's slippers

My grandfather had as a youth
a pair of bright slippers
and he went up and down

on the pavement, in the office
and through the train,

wearing them. And people looked
and looked away
and hid behind their papers
and peeped over the top.

Those slippers were
bright and hard and
a little bit scandalous. It's not
right he ought to keep them

under his hat, they said.

But when he sat
his knees in a warped grey blanket
spilling ash
my grandfather
was glad he had them.

Anamorphic Woman

'Who is it?' 'Who is it?'
'Woman or weapon?'

Medusa with her snakey hair.

Ah.

'Look at her!' 'Look at her!' 'No, don't - !'

'Does she turn me to stone?' 'She'll turn me to stone!'
'My bloods and my pulses will all cease to flow.'

'She shouldn't be showing - they shouldn't be seen.'
'Snake in the green! Snake in the green!'

'Kill her!' 'Let's kill her!'
Then she'll be useful, then she'll be clean.'

'A weapon is what she will be.'

So that all other
snake women
had better take care?

'He could turn them to stone, then.' 'Yes, he could.'
        'Yes, he will.' 'A lot of stone women!'
'How good! Ah, how good!'

'The snakeheads, all living - I had to kill each.
I used the thin moon, like a knife, sharp and keen,
        which I filched from the sky.'
'How many, Perseus?' 'What are the figures?'
'I rather lost count - lots, that is all.- And, whatever I
        killed, there grew more and more.
They all have to go - we must stamp them out, all.'

'Why did you kill her? Why, Perseus, why?'
'Well you know - when a man sees a snake - it's a
            matter of honour - he's driven by gods.
They gave me *furor*. It wasn't inside me
till they put it there.'

'But did the snakes mind?' 'Are you out of your mind?
A snake is a snake, it's a fact, look, look at her, look.
            They don't petrify me.
But they will their own kind.'

'Who is it?' 'Who is it?'
'Woman or weapon?'

Just tilt the woman. Or just tilt your head. Now.
            Have you done it? Have you shifted
                  perspective?

'She's a looker from this angle.' 'A looker.' 'She looks'

She lives
a respectable, neighbourly citizen
and reads all the papers
on Sunday till noon.

O.

Pan and Syrinx understood

After the story falls a pregnant hush.
A meaning must be found; there is a need
to find out why the nymph became a reed
and why the god grasped flesh that made a rush.

Perhaps the meaning is he was inspired
by loving her, to introduce an art;
or nymph is rite, and reed religion's heart;
or nymph is river, he Nature, by which rush is sired.

The tale congeals, assuming crust on crust;
the nymph, the god, the reed, relinquish awe,
the body of the story lost, transformed to straw,
joyful exposure dancing into rust.

Pope, you were right, but what you said indeed
was, *Fools rush in where angels fear to read.*

I am writing a poem

I'm writing a poem;
but I noticed, as I came to my desk,
that the lampshades
haven't been dusted for seven years.

I'm writing a poem;
and I saw, when I ransacked the cupboard,
that there aren't any dusters
of the right type.

So I go back to the poem;
but then I ought to go and buy some dusters;
and dust the lampshades;
so I do.
There's a long queue at the check-out.

I've dusted the lampshades;
but now there are long grey tendrils
and blobs and gobbets of dust
on the carpet I hoovered this morning.
So I'll have to get the hoover out again.

Now I'm writing a poem;
but I really ought to open out the hoover,
while I think of it,
and just check that the filters aren't all clogged up.
It might be too late before I remember again.

All done. I'm writing a poem about -
but when I was looking for the dusters
I found that the cupboard was awkwardly stuffed
with all sorts of things I don't need.

Time to have a clear-out.

Paul Coleman

Paul Coleman

When he's not peeping up the skirts of academia, Paul Coleman writes, plays the guitar and adores his wife Sandra. In his spare time he is a plaything for cats.

Fireworks at Port de Chôlet

Over traceries of inlets, the night bloomed,
tumbled, slowly, slowly, on our heads.
By holy pyromania consumed,
we gaped and gasped by the mussel beds.

Eyes full of fire from the molten sky,
we opened mussels under countless suns.
Blood-drum echoed each boom and sigh,
with salt and sulphur on our tongues.

We watched heaven torn by stabbing shoots
and imprison in our eyes a searing flower.
Above our heads - but also in our roots -
the old surprise at our own power.

Bempton Cliffs

White cliffs crack and crumble in slow time, as
a thousand seabirds tumble in the crusty air.
Perching puffins like affable uncles blink, while
needle-beaked herring gulls yak and caw.

A constant, discordant symphony in flight spins
around us. Ages before us it was here.
Puffins shuffle their feet, avert their gaze.
Guillemots and gannets show no measure of surprise.

In an unchanging but always-shifting vista,
which writhed thus for the first son of man
to see it on an egg-quest long ago, staring
puffins fall soundless from their ledges.

Set in Stone

No hallowed halls these, just enough
concrete to make the soul ache
and the eye shy, half in sorrow,
half in wincing pique.
To think a shiny seat of learning
could be worn so shabby new.

No stately edifice, or painted ceiling,
encompasses our thoughts.
They drift away forever
through the ill-fitting frames
of windows and of doors.
They scuttle down metal mouseholes.

We own no holy chapel. No
stained glass colours our ideas.
Our never-followed rituals
were hatched amidst the scum upon
the surface of a nineteen-sixties
think tank's rank and dismal overflow.

We do have a lake here, though it
is man-made and full of decoy ducks.
It laps against the banks of learning,
churning with sick pike and
rusting shopping trolleys sinking
into their own pre-formed oblivion.

Dead Lodgers

You didn't fly south, you dropped from the eaves,
All feathered together in your little nest.
A moment's fluttering autumn ecstacy
Led you to freeze with your tardy brood.
They came too late, the young ones;
African skies won't fill their eyes.

We thought you'd gone to the sun,
Until the nest fell, broke open.
Avian aliens in your downy craft,
You plummeted in blue plumage,
Little eyes closed before the launch:
First flight for them, last flight for you.

Mrs Martin and the children – didn't you hear?
They stood no chance in the grim chill:
Waiting, waiting for the wings to form.
Open mouths with no flies to eat.
Hanging on in a silent huddle
'Til their world fell into flightlessness.

Pornic Market, July 15th

At Pornic market, rain rinsed aromas around
as we did the old shoulder dance.

Roast meat and spices tugged our sleeves.
At Pornic market, we weaved like petit-point:

sun-red, pink or white from night before.
Local lingo trickled in our ears.

At Pornic market, parasols were suddenly sodden,
the Grande Creme tasted like hot spit.

We sat and shrugged and steamed.
At Pornic market, we tried to buy things:

but patterns eluded us and there was too much cheese.
The only thing that reached us was the rain.

At Pornic market, we stopped no more to look.
Water washed us to the bottom of the hill.

We might have salmon-leaped back up
but at Pornic market we gathered in the depths,

lingering no longer in its shallow gaze;
Pornic market poised above our heads.

La Cat

Saddle-up my hummingbird hawk moth.
Give the sun a polish; shine the flowers.
Turn up the volume on the sparrows - if you will.
Waft a bit more lavender my way.

Saddle-up my hummingbird hawk moth.
Let the bees buzz somewhere over there.
Turn down the contrast on the pool - just a little.
Leave the trees to rustle, that's okay.

Saddle-up my hummingbird hawk moth.
Give the sun a polish; shine the flowers.
Turn up the volume on the birdies a bit more
and slow the hours, slow the hours, slow the hours.

Folklorique at Bois de Céné

See them dance
    the old and young
hear their music
    catch their tongue
rough their clothes
    but bonnet lace
treasure-troves
    of lines on face
lines of Dancers
    old and young
blushing prancers
    shy unsung
rhythm-stepping
    lost in time
see the dancers
    line on line
let them dance
    not old young
let the music
    drown their tongue
keep their clothes
    and bonnet lace
treasure troved
    in hiding place
lines of dancers
    old not young
courting couples
    centuries gone
rhythm-stepping
    caught in time
see the prancing
    feet in line
never-ending rhythm's chance
    see them dance
   see them dance

Grey Goddess

Sick grey goddess, leaden skies,
scavengers paw-apart your
grubby death-rags.
Plastic radio, summer haze:
dropped concrete heart
begins to throb.

Acolytes tramp your flanks
and crack your drying flesh.
Prayers exude from orifices
but they never ever
look you in the face.
Mother-haters.

Dogs prowl, holy bowels,
cats are in the sanctity.
Monkey-boys split your bones.
Prostrate in offerings,
drunk priests flout their power:
crack no smile.

Melanie Duckworth

Melanie Duckworth

Melanie Duckworth was born in England in 1979, but has lived most of her life in Australia. She returned to the UK in 2003 for postgraduate study in medieval literature at the universities of York and Leeds. Her first collection of poetry, *Triangular Light*, was published in 2002. Her poetry and short stories appear in various journals in Australia, and she is currently finishing her first novel.

Paraclete

You would like a poem about a bird,
about *that* bird
which is a deeper grey than pigeons,
is delicate,
and is visiting our feet.
We do not know what kind it is
but there is something lovely
about grey wings which sheathe
realms of air beneath their quiet feathers,
about the pointed bright eyed head
which bows and bobs
and knows something, but will not say.

Apart from that
it is a bird, and birds
have soft breasts we long to touch
but cannot own –
brittle underneath and light as air,
warm quickly pulsing
(our groping hands would crush in loving
or die of gentleness)
– and mostly, a presence
which can dip away in half a second
but is near now.

I would like to build a nest with words
(nothing like a cage)
fine enough and firm enough
for the bird to live close to you.

You could carry her around like a good secret,
you could take her out at night.

She would diminish the darkness
but you still wouldn't own her:
the bird would be just as precious
just as rare, pure gift.

Moonless Night

The Milky Way rainbows above us;
you say it is a weak name
for such a glory.
The sea is one shade of charcoal
darker than the sky
and we cannot even see the island –
only the lighthouses
are stars pinning sky to sea
and there is land
across the water.

Living there alone, climbing stairs and keeping
lamps burning in turning towers,
not speaking or seeing anyone for months,
you would not know the other beacon
at the island's far rim
but they speak to us together and say
here is an island.

Grass that was gold in late afternoon
has folded the colour of wheat
into the colour of night.
If I curled up like a stone on this hillside, I would be
as real as the hill, as solid and as old,
as unquestionable as wallabies in the shifting dark.

Walking a narrow path between all that grey
I take my hand out of my pocket;
you catch it, and we walk inside the grey night
wrapped in sea and stars.
Holding hands, not looking at flocks of questions
or the old hurts which come again
as if through channels in rock,
not speaking, knowing
our worlds touch but spin
with loneliness of different keys.

For a moment inside and so not needing
words which divide
sea from sky, wallaby from stone,
our questions from the gentle night.

The world, the island
exist, whether I believe in them or not,
the round hills still cradle, bear us.
Apart from this, I do not know
what is real or what I want, only we long
to be lights at the edge of the sky
shining and fading and shining
inside the blurred dark horizon, saying
there is land here
across the water.

Once

You hardly knew me
but kissed my head and sighed
as though you'd found a home amongst my hair.
Never being anyone's home before
I leant into you,
and we became for an hour
earth's tenderness.

Outside the darkening window,
the city moved.
Our pasts and futures whirled around us
and didn't come in –
they couldn't pass your warm breath
sleeping on my neck.

The memory is distracting and so must go –
I will take it for a long walk by the river
I will let it go
along the gleaming river, cold in twilight.

To Spring

You've been wooing me for days,
invisibly, with the most delicate of whispers.
With a fragrant smell despite the clouds,
with sunlight on my bathroom floor,
with snowdrops crowding the tombstones
of the old church.
I'm pretending not to notice,
knowing (rightly) that winter will crush me again,
hammer me with black weight,
and I am so tired.

How can I trust what weighs less than my breathing
and vanishes when I turn around?

But look, winter's worn himself out with gravity
and there's nothing to do
but breathe again, and float upwards.
I had read of the lightness of spring
but never felt it –
this quiet buoyancy – how strange!
O fickle lover, I know you won't stay.
Now it's birdcalls in the mornings,
and minute gifts of extra daylight,
and everything will rise again without trying,
impossibly.

I won't speak of you yet, too loudly –
I might scare you away.

Yes, cold may come again,
with the wind and the hail,
but maybe I trust you,
maybe I like you,
maybe I'll walk with you, now.

Blondes

He liked blondes.
This was why, at first, he talked to me,
testing his most charming lines –
the paragon of courtesy.

Perceiving a lost cause before too long
he moved on to the other one
(not as tall but just as nice)
whose straight hair wisped and shone.

Its honey deepened in his gaze,
her doe face glowed, but it wasn't to be –
just two weeks later, lounging on the lawn,
I saw him with blonde number three.

Behold the longest locks (and fairest) of us all –
a veritable ringlet waterfall.
Her slim arm curved across his back
then curled around his knee.

Not my type, I thought again, and it was true,
but envied them, just then, that easy grace –
the feathered sun, the yellow air
brilliant in her pale hair.

Eve

My name is an exotic flower in your mouth
I taste its strange new petals on your tongue.

'There must be poems about this,' you say.
'There are,' I say, 'and good ones too.'

'No, this – the moonlight on your lover's breast –
whoever designed it got it right.'

And I am glad to be a body, warm and smooth
for light to sculpt, for hands to stroke.

I watch the grey dawn gather in your eyes
and need no other sun

as though I were a creature formed from your rib,
named only by your tongue.

And we finally allow ourselves to sleep
only for the pleasure of waking

still whole.

Clarissa Ford

Clarissa Ford

Clarissa Ford was born in Essex in 1978. She studied for her first degree in English at the University of York before taking the MA in Creative Writing at the University of East Anglia. In 2001, she undertook a PGCE and currently works in a large Sixth Form College in Essex teaching Curriculum 2000 and the International Baccalaureate.

The Blue Pool

for Francis Bacon

Stretching up to dive into this blue pool,
your vertical body curves like a half-moon
through its shadow.

This blue would fill you,
blot and dissolve you into lighter things,
too small for language.

Its surface is frantic;
gull-hungry thoughts paddle
as you draw me up through the edge
that positions you.

I am a simple frame with translucent lines
that fix squarely around this sinking hull.

I give you perspective; containment,
and as I breathe your shadow steadies,
curling as you fold as cleanly as a cat lick to touch
water.

You call to love and carefully cup her,
as if newborn
in your halved hands. She calms you,

her delicate warmth
stretching above the outline of blue
that used to be
your touch.

Tights

At this moment in time, spoilt for choice,
I act casually, natural: naturally normal and indecisive.
I am careful not to disturb this fragile order of things:
Lace, silk, beige, black, barely black.

At this moment in time, as I stroke the puffed packets
I can feel your eyes holding my flexed hands,
their gloved fingers systematically folding,
as if spoiling dominoes.

But at this moment in time I can imagine
the long yawn as you stretch a leg into these
to begin dressing. One leg stepping up the bed
then pushing down, cutting the floor sharply as if
                working a spade.

And at this moment in time, you seem aware of my
                intentions,
complicit in this act you walk away to serve.
I hear the punctuated crack of your heels
and the teasing chafe of your thighs.

At the Bus Stop

Your cheeks bellow in
as the red spark of your cigarette
draws inland.

Hiding my gaze,
the rings on your fingers slowly
weight your hand down.

I wonder,
if I made a mask of your face,
could I pull each perfect line?

That thick slap of pink across your lips?

Woman in the Waiting Room

On the tight leather sofa
I wait to be called in.

With little interest in the magazines,
I focus on the pleat of your skirt

and that static rush
of your tights,

as you cross and uncross,
and cross and uncross.

Erigone

for Icarius

If I had a child
I would place her in a tree
to grow strong and sturdy.
I would see to that.

Set above the ground
she could learn the stars,
take the divine path
with air as her sign.

But if one day, I should find
her dead; I would bury her
beneath this tree,
fallen as fruit.

My evergreen girl,
who taught the birds to call
a piercing shriek.
If I had a child.

The Boat

The moon is shrouding them in lace,
her lens of absent colour refracted through the cabin
        window,
a spotlight for the alphabet of faint sounds that push
from his lips.

This is the third day sailing, the third night waves have
patterned
the walls with hieroglyphs,
gannets diving at right angles like slight crosses,
        dropping
feathered bullets.

She wipes him with a damp cloth,
hardly recognising his new geography,
each feature planed and faded,
falling through him with horizons.

These shadows leave her no answer,
ephemeral shapes she cannot make out.
So she prays for light, to hide the infrared that rhythms
        through him,
visible as if his skin had been peeled back,
his veins pumping dry with brine.

Song

for Maria Callas

Your image opens like a pedal bin,
hatched out colourless inside of me.
Echoes drip from my ears
without space enough to hold you.

Through thick mascara your pupils dilate
as if they were your voice,
the air that keeps you paced,
this vibrating throat that topples me.

I waver, feeling sure I'll drop,
as the breath I need to pull me back
is held, held, held,
held against the puffed breve of your lips.

River Death

It was here beside the fountain she found him washing,
floating his white linen
among the lily pads, anchored and reflecting a cool
            dark stain.

'I could fit your pieces together,
that giant knuckle between your hip,
just let me get beyond it' she whispered.

And if you listen carefully, you can hear she's on him,
the lily pads pulled under,
white linen festering among weeds.

Dave Gough

Dave Gough

Dave Gough has declined the opportunity to give autobiographical details in a vain attempt to cultivate an air of mystery.

This Scepter'd Isle

Donkey rides and flower show fetes,
In the rain,
In the rain.
Ham and egg picnics with paper plates,
In the rain,
In the rain.
Bank holiday gridlock yet again,
In the rain,
In the rain.

And at Headingly, Yorkshire are 63 for 4.
Rain stopped play.
(Pitch inspection at 4.30).

Long Friday PM

What use was $\pi (R - r) (R + r)$
To the average 14 year old?
None.
Not then, not now,
Nor at any time in between.

As time ground to a halt
I gazed longingly upon
The smooth parabolic curves
Of Miss Webber's
Newly qualified, nubile body.
I assessed the circumference
Of her waist
And pondered upon
The ratio 36 : 24 : 36.
I considered
And weighed up
The volume of her breasts
(rough reckoning suggested
perhaps 700cc).

That was $\frac{1}{2}$ a lifetime ago.
Now I've got 2· 4 kids,
15·9 APR and 90k of mortgage.
Rose must be pushing 60 now
And I doubt whether her pupils
Still lust after her.
So, I suppose the poor little bastards
Will be left with nothing but
$\pi (R - r) (R + r)$
On a Friday afternoon.

Interesting But...

Hanging valleys, ox-bow lakes,
Frogspawn, newts, extinct Corncrakes.
Diagrams of diatoms,
Jules, amperes and mega ohms.

The members of the EEC,
Specific heat capacity.
The 23 irregular verbs,
Australia's most deadly herbs.
                    What a waste of time.

The Boll Weevil's biology,
And terminal velocity.
The breed of horses in Camargue,
Defenestrations in old Prague.

The flagship of a great Armada,
Harolds Godwinson and Hardrada,
The making of a modern nation,
And forces of acceleration.
                    What a waste of time.

The South Sea Bubble - why it burst,
Tudors, James and Charles the First,
The siege of London's Sidney Street,
Converting metres into feet.

The square on the hypotenuse,
The lack of scurvy in Cook's crews.
Damascus, dirt roads and Saint Paul,
The fact that Hitler had one ball.
                    What a waste of time.

Livingstone and Captain Scott,
What's magnetic and what's not.
All these things I learned at school,
While smoking ciggies; looking cool.
What a waste of time.

What a waste of time?

Daddy, You Know Animals...

Daddy,
Do laughing hyenas have lots of fun?
Will butterflies melt if left in the sun?
Do cheetahs cheat? Does an octopus purr?
Do all lions lie and do bears have fur?
Do boks have springs and tell me what's a gnu?
And if moo cows moo will poodles shit poo?
    Ey, I've told you about that!

Do congers dance and will a sad porcu pine?
Does a slow loris ponder when taking his time?
Do antelopes all have nephews and nieces?
Will a tiger rip you into small pieces?

Do spiders spy? Can adders multiply?
Teacher doesn't know but I'm sure they try.
Are all badgers bad and do panthers panth?
And what kind of fish is a coelacanth?
Daddy,
DADDY...

Go and ask your mother, she'll know.

Tabloid Times

Bash Trash Smash
  Knock Rock
    Slate Bait Hate
      Trumpet Strumpet
        Blight Slight Shite.

Hype Snipe Gripe
  Hack Flack
    Tease Grease Sleaze
      Tits Shits
        Moan Groan Stone.

Joke Poke Stoke
  Rage Stage
    Bleat Cheat Beat
      Accuse Confuse
        Spy Buy Lie.

Gotcha.

To Oscar (November 30th 2000)

Bit of a bugger really;
the way they treated you
all that time ago.
It would be different
today. Probably.
Most of the time.

But
it would depend on
where you lived,
and who you talked to.
So, it's a
bit of a bugger really.

Thus Passes The Glory Of The World

Sick and incapable in a
Transit van with
Gloria on a wet
Monday night.

The Home Front

From the wardrobe behind the door
to the linen basket under the window
an iron curtain has descended across the bedroom.
I fear it is the beginning of the end,
for never, in the field of domestic finance
was so much owed to so many by so few.
I said 'I have nothing to offer
but blood, toil, tears and sweat.'
It seems this was not enough.
So, we shall go on to the end,
we shall fight with growing bitterness,
we shall defend our positions whatever the cost may be.
We shall argue in the kitchen, we shall argue in the hall,
we shall argue in the car and in the bathroom,
we shall argue in the supermarket and in the street,
we shall never stop arguing.
I begged my legal advisors to
'Give me the tools and I will finish the job,
because this is the sort of treatment
up with which I shall not put.
The whole fury and might of my wife
must soon be turned upon us,
yet if we can stand up to this
then life may move forward into broad sunlit uplands.
But if we fail then the world,
including all that I have cared for
will sink into the abyss of a new dark age.
I cannot forecast to you the actions of my wife,
she is a riddle wrapped in a mystery inside an enigma.
But it is separation at all costs,
separation in spite of all the terror,
separation however long and hard the road may be;
for without it there is no survival.'

There can be no doubt; this is not our finest hour.

Post Match Analysis

Well Brian on the night it was a typical cup tie, a game of two halves played at 100 mph from the word go and the atmosphere was electric.

PHENOMENAL.

Very much so.

The weather was against us but the pitch played great, to be fair they've come out and given us a game, we've gave away a silly goal but the ball took a wicked deflection.

IMMENSE.

Very much so.

We've got men in the box, behind the ball, round the back and up the middle. The fouls were cynical the crosses were super and the finishing clinical.

IMMACULATE.

Very much so.

We've moved the ball around and got a result, at the end of the day the lads done brilliant, the support was magnificent and its been a great advert for English football in general. We're over the moon Brian.

UNREAL.

Very much so.

Amy Rootvik

Amy Rootvik

Amy Rootvik is a part-time instructor of English and Gender Studies. In the last three years, she has read at poetry events and has taught creative writing workshops in the United Kingdom and the United States. Amy received her MA in Women's Studies from the University of York in 2003. She has since returned home to Washington State.

5:52pm on Boyer Avenue

I stop and park the car to catch
the perfect slant of light. A couple cross
the street casting lean shadows over amber
and crimson leaves. At the base of tree trunks
halos in reverse mark autumn's shift.
Green has turned and dropped to the ground. A gown
slipped off the shoulders at the end of the party
falls, lies around the ankles, feet
with strappy heels like timid roots. And the trees
will leave these garments to insulate their veins
until a blanket of snow takes their place.
Through the winter they will work undercover.
They'll suck those fallen clothes under the ground,
draw them up through veins, and in the spring
press them out again, renewed and green
for the annual summer dance.
                              Today I grab
my camera to capture perfect light
full of bugs and mystery, of romance
and the smell of harvest. By the time
I step out of the car, image eager,
the sun has dropped too low, too shy for me
to coax her out. Perhaps the nearly nude
tree-dancers requested lowered lights.

Beverly Beach

The beach found us after dark, halfway down
the Oregon Coast. Water touched the sand –
a tidal lover in retreat, breathing
in the starlight power in the pullback.
We walked a hundred yards from our tent site
followed pacing beams of handheld torches

under a bridge where weary drivers chased
electric moonbeams on tarmacadam.
Sea mist filled our lungs & eyes. On our hands
& knees we dug sand, grit coating palms,
lodging under nails. Around the hole, rocks
made the spot our fire fortress. Sheltered sparks

crawled thru logs, grew into white & orange,
blazed under the brightest milky way
we'd seen in months. Fog cleared from heads & sky.
Of course we had to tempt the night ocean,
Mother Pacific. Feet pounded across sand
to play tag with shallow surf. Maybe it

was the shooting star that set me off
but I knew I had to feel her force,
the press of her waves against me.
After midnight I ran into the surf,
dove under the surface 30 feet off shore,
felt the push & pull – saltwater body.

Cold cramped my chest; my feet were nearly numb.
Blood pumped & my heart gripped
as waves hit sand behind my starlit crawl
stroke, hand over hand splash breaking the line
between ocean & air. Breathless at night.
Others soon joined me in the rush, feeling

the weight & power of her massive form.
Walking cold & wet back onto dry land
I was glad for the fire still burning.
I stood beside its warmth, saltwater dried
on flesh. Hair hung like seaweed by a smile
& my heart almost returned.

A February Date (On Friday the 13th)

She says, "I want to date you."
What defines dating, then?
Promises not in the cards.
My father told me never to play
poker – full house on Valentine's.

I sleep in her bed, arms wrap
around her labour hardened torso.
We wake with swollen eyes.
Was this a date?

Dinner & dancing. But we dance
in her two-room flat
where ghosts & allergens
reach up from the floor,
deaden senses & swell limbs.

Ghost-Dance

We dance in her two-room flat
where ghosts & allergens
reach up from the floor,
deaden senses & swell limbs.

I hold her close for slow –
slow – slow-fast-slow
steps around an oak coffee table
where half-drunk tea turns cold.

The spirit of us grows weak.
Limbs try to follow, hearts fail to lead.
When music stops & arms drop
to our sides, the must in the air

& the glimmer by candlelight
prove the angel of our love has expired.
Ghost-life glances and late-night dances
cannot resurrect old truths.

I lift my grief-stained head,
raise a tired hand as in toast
to bless the ghost of fairytale romance,
to tell an old lover I must go.

There's a train in forty minutes.
Breath clouds trail like smoke
on my walk across town to the station
          & away from tranquillising hope.

What To Do With Shadows

Her train pulls up to Platform 3 –
time for me to run alongside,
make faces in the window
as she settles into virgin cushions,
laughs at antics, pulls away
after a final hug. She
looks forward to another
town, another woman.
Late sunlight presses through portholes
in brick walls – blue spheres
held by gold crescents and shadows.
The slant of light holds longing
just above my reach & casts long
hearts on flagstones and leaves.
Her sadness burns my eyes.
Emptiness, space I once filled,
expands as we move apart. Maybe
she knows something I can't see, blinded
by white sky & heat waves from bodies
in the cold. It's hollow here –
walk away as the train pulls out
carriage by carriage, separates my hand
from hers. Someone else waits for her,
loves her, has done her laundry
while she's been here dancing with me.

We danced last night & talked & sang.
We moved until eyes closed
and bodies cried, but our bodies cried
for different things. She slept
in a guest bed
I lay in mine – fitful,
holding ghosts, the curve
of her back against my chest. Maybe
she dreamed of flowing skirts,
black velvet jackets and red curls

running through her fingers –
mouth to mouth more passionate
when forbidden. She will pull away.
The tricks she plays on herself. She'll say
she doesn't want it cheap, must work
harder for the intimacy she craves.
Self-fulfilling prophecies of solitude.
She runs, rides many rails and
bends away from longing.

Tomorrow She Flies

Tomorrow she flies
to town across the open bay
to set the headstone
on her grandparents' grave.
She won't be alone.
But now, lying
in her grandparents' old bed
under the weight of a quilt
she made when she was nine
and her grandfather's wool
army blanket from WWII,
she feels the weight of solitude.
The outgoing tide disrobes
untracked silty plains,
glassy reflectors
of the sky's changing moods.
Tonight, dark & wet.
Mosquitoes swarm,
building grey-black
auras about all who stay
still for a moment
in the damp night air.

Patrick Smith

Patrick Smith

After an early incarnation as a fitter / turner in the engineering industry, Patrick Smith returned to college as a mature student, embarking on an odyssey which would see him pursue the very personal goal of becoming a Fine Artist. Since leaving Art College in the late 90s, Patrick has become established both as a lecturer in further education, teaching at several colleges, and as a practising fine artist printmaker. His interest in the spoken word and in particular performance poetry has seen him develop a wry and at times comedic observation of life, tempered with good old fashioned Yorkshire cynicism.

Cretan Nights

Warm air, scent of olive groves.
Bleach wizened bracken, crystal under foot.
Salt air dancing on the tongue, blown
hard around the coast.

Hands clasped to the tune of trippers,
sanitised explorers thirsting for difference
halted at the beauty of the mundane, elevated
to some holiday importance.

Rich aromas punctuate evening's shroud
as back lit menus service the crowd.
Languages merge and join, unified to the sound
of alfresco munching, and the native scratch
of crickets.

Old Jack

Revolving hardness, centrifugal energy,
anchored, tamed, offered possibilities, submissive
to the cut, surfaces excavated, checked, measured.

A turner's eye, feelings learned, honed
on an anvil of experience, apprenticed to knowledge,
        realised
within the closed reality of the machine shop.
Ink and manila; clock no. seventy-one.

Old Jack, long dead. Factory
closed for the day. Held court forty years,
a majestic union, man and machine, nimble
hands dancing on levers, but no more.

His *amour* of knowledge passed to the few. I
had the best of him, and for one day the lathes stopped
turning. He loved his pigeons.

Upright Push & Shove

Gilly wants a cleaner, upright push and shove.
She's got a Vax but can't relax, it's not the one she
loves.
There's rows and rows of models, all pristine, spic-and-
span,
But Dyson's got an aqualung and three-speed turbo
fan.

'Can I try a demo, take this cheap one on a trial?'
Shake and vac then hand it back, it stands out by a
mile.
'But will it pick the dirt up, my kitchen floor's a mess?
Vindaloo meets Quatermass – I'll put it to the test.'

And so the battle started: Round One, it's suck and
blow,
Lego brick and Weatabix – the motor's running slow.
'I wonder what that smell is that permeates the air?'
A long forgotten sandwich emerges from a chair.

Round Two, the school bell's ringing, the kids all run
amuck,
Trampling Bourbon biscuits, mud and yoghurt on the
rug,
Like a predatory pride of lions against a lonesome
bison,
She says, 'Keep your crap, I'll hand it back, cos' all I
want's a Dyson!'

I wish

I wish I were Arnold Schwartzenegger, fighting the
    scum and decay
Out on the streets with impossible feats; the man with
    the military beret.
I wish I were Tom Cruise, up in the heavens, flying the
    American flag;
Nine o'clock high, grit in my eye and a Russian Mig in
    the bag.

But I am not a Hollywood idol as I leave the cinema
    queue
Inflated, sedated and much overrated; synthetic, not
    honest or true.
My name is Patrick anonymous, blended, not shaken
    or stirred,
I move in salubrious circles, yet I'm very much part of
    the herd.

Give me command of the Enterprise, beam me down
    when the going gets tough,
I could dock with a good-looking alien, then save the
    planet from stuff.
I still hold my mouth when the Marathon Man is
    drilled and his teeth start to bleed,
Take me back to the time of *The Graduate*, Mrs
    Robinson, I'm begging you please.

My world was *Saturday Swap Shop*, Noel Edmunds and
    Morecambe & Wise,
Z Cars was on at eight-thirty, *Tomorrow's World* was a
    constant surprise,
Pan's People would dance with no clothes on (a
    schoolboy's erotic wet dream).
Do you remember *Top of the Pops* albums? Real artists
    (or so it would seem).

Oh, how I long for those halcyon days of beans on
        toast when I came home from school.
Mud were the kings with 'Tiger Feet', at the blonde
        girl from ABBA I'd drool,
Everyone wore scoop-necked cheesecloths, denims
        were faded and flared,
Doctor Who came on with some Yetis, behind settees
        we quivered and stared.

A lifetime of thoughts in a jumble, of echoes and ties
        from the past,
When the popcorn has gone and Rank bangs his gong,
feelings and memories last.

Never Change

I'm sat thinking of you.
A smile flows from glamorous eyes, headstrong
in notions of being. You sit dragging life
from narcotic solutions, expectantly squeezed
between newly applied, going home lipstick.

The philosophy of the hard shift, the day to day
hospital realities of the maternity ward, eased
by conversation, the gossip of acceptance,
decanted to a glass of chilled white wine.

I'm sat listening to you.
So full of life. So full
of existence tempered by the maturity
of innocence. Never change.
Never change.

The Void

Shards of twisted metal rising from the ashes,
Patriotic sound-bites feed the bloodlust masses.

Hope and reason vanquished, depression fills the void,
Where buildings stood, crushed souls and blood,
Real life, not celluloid.

Skimmer

Your eyes bear out the searching
fixed on life beyond,
your heart a well-worn pebble
that skims across a pond.
All too brief, you've filled my world,
your smile and caring charm
bring tempest winds of energy
to my dormant soul becalmed.

Walls can hold an essence,
my mind the musk of love,
the growing sense of knowingness.
The hand sheathed by the glove,
thresholds gently merging,
disparate feelings fused,
inner thoughts, collected dreams,
and fantasies unused.

I'm Being Stalked by Naomi Campbell

I have something to say which is a bit of a gamble:
I'm being stalked by Naomi Campbell.
I was in Tesco's the other day near the frozen peas,
Naomi came over trying to put me at ease,
I said, 'what are you doing? Why are you here?'
She said, 'calm down, my darling, I just want to be
      near.'
I'm being stalked by Naomi Campbell.

She wants me to travel and be by her side,
Luxury yachts and lear-fan jets,
But give me Hunmanby Gap and a Filey high tide,
She wouldn't like Skeggie, that's a fair bet.
I said, 'it wouldn't work out, Naomi, you're all over the
      place;
Paris, Milan, New York en route.
I've an old Nissan Micra, so I couldn't commute.'
I'm being stalked by Naomi Campbell.

But Naomi is dogged and doesn't give up,
'I'll pay for the petrol and whatever you sup.'
This sweet talking vision and media queen
Was making suggestions that were clearly obscene.
I'm being stalked by Naomi Campbell.

I'd have to give up all that I know, my two-up-two-
      down,
My job at the meat processing plant,
And a couple of pubs I frequent in the town.
Please, Naomi, leave me in peace.
I've got prostate trouble and old age to look forward
      to;
It would be a release.
Why can't you be with your glamorous friends,
Having wild parties and setting new trends?
I'm being stalked by Naomi Campbell.

Waiting for me at the factory gates
Is causing me problems with all of my mates.
They're totally jealous and want to know why
You constantly ring and give me the eye.
I'm being stalked by Naomi Campbell.

Nicolas Spicer

Nicolas Spicer

Nicolas Spicer had the misfortune to get born in Kent, but has been drifting northwards towards civilisation ever since. Having spent most of the past decade in York, he currently lives in Newcastle-upon-Tyne, where he indulges in a wide range of vices, including but not limited to beer, cigarettes and poetry.

Black Light Songs

The boys are back in town.
Time has got faster on them.

April.
The city
drips.

The pavements are running with water
& down at the Hope & Anchor

it's time for a pint.

†

What price
roadtrips

when here are duty & the future
& us come so close?

Look how we slide.

Greased down this evening
into black light
ourselves

wrapped up in us like
old clothes
bad jokes.

†

Our strained voices
whispering

under a mechanical
storm of singing

bang on the heartbeat.
Everything we have is put to use.

Eyes clutching. Hands
shifting in time.

†

This place is brilliant.
On show unseen & everyone

waving roundglitteringeyed
at some

thing away out there. Everyone
sweating & dirty-sweet.

To step outside at sunrise. To bathe
in clean water.

†

Six in the morning. The house
is a beautiful mess.

These decent people
my people

have the loud inglorious night
a very little vision

obscene & subtle
limbs & morals.

†

Our joys in kind are still
not unlike the first

in quality
well memory is caustic
for now.

We paid for what we wanted
not highly
but enough & disremember

the how
of given taking.

†

Well we can say where we been
or thereabouts.

We have been approximately
in flight.

Falling's alright it's when you
stop.

Pollen

Youth's a stuff will not endure.
(Twelfth Night, II.iii)

In a paradise, now,
the sneezing starts again with a bang: it's been
away but it goes it comes back to set your eyes
running, nose on trickle, mucous membranes
      affronting awareness
& everything wants to be given attention or paid
court: the summer flowers are out & the bees
are taking them for special friends, yeah
it's that time of the year & just like some sort of
      infection
        here we go:
the trees have bedroom hair, the nettles & grasses
are randy it being the season & using the air for a
      brothel,
milady sweetandtwenty-eight, perspiration-jewelled &
      all,
        well, legs,
something is wrong with this picture but that's okay,
there's a rubber in my top pocket & Feste was right,
        it won't endure,
not yet, but if we grew up to indulge those youthful
fond ideas about love, perhaps we'd fall
together not ill & come to sketch ourselves
        flowering forever.

Climate Is What You Expect

August & thunderheads & the flying ants
coming into the dry, & dying.

        They have been kings,
glorifying this day with suits of lights
hastily put together; now they rest,
consorted with exhaustion, glaucous wings
twitching the muzzy air.

        Their little ends
crawl on the ground underfoot, a rain of love.

The Ecstasy

In the event, two lifetime's heaviness
compacts itself to neutrons, & there's us
watching the humans do their human thing,

all of them beautiful, all of them: girls & boys
shaping their mouths for friendliness, their eyes
opening to each other; then there's us,

sky-high & plummeting up to our orbits, us
out of our minds to come as close as this,
us two in our naked singularity, all-attractive.

consequence

leave

don't know what you'd say but I reckon
the weather's getting weird—

thirteenth of December
12 degrees—

you close enough
to feel your body's warmth

far enough
not to see the pores in your skin—

so many absolutely clean
surfaces in the room
but who really remembers

                       snow—
what it looked like in quantity—

the colour it went
melting trodden in the streets—

everything good goes away

temper temper

still it's a bloody good day that the sun gets a look-in

so Town Moor afternoons
                              is melted sulphur
the cows in it up to their knees—
                                  & the birds
sing a sodium vapour chorus at 2 a.m.

just at the hibernating moment—
                                  while lovers
are loudly creating on the street
                              (not already
exciting enough for each other)
dramatic circumstances

stupid stupid stupid

and if we were need
                         shaking for an answer
beyond each other
                         but only learnt the art
of ending up
                those red sky days—
our histories
                their bloodwarm myths—
not much to look at later—

                        forget
tripping up Dog Leap Stairs in a cloud of laughter
for the promise of frost
                         blowing across the moon—
scribbles refined to a vanishing point—

& seen from this distance
we are songs

from The Ballad of Tom the Rhymer

1. Last Night

Meanwhile, back at the wateringhole, there's a
            dilemma —
lager or stout? — for the exquisite fauns, the jackals,
the bloodygreat hippos, hyenas being jocular
& grouchy lions with serotonin problems.

It's too late at night & no-one can find their still centre,
the Siamese couples are coming to separations;
the peaceful jostling round the refreshment counter
disintegrates into fights & accusations:

— You're only ever beautiful when you're drunk,
you're only ever beautiful when *I'm* drunk,
we're not in love just justabout in lust —

which makes it a pretty good time to pick up & slink
            off,
still grinning, having swallowed quite enough
of other people's clots of second-best.

3. Born Reader

Tom dreams of courage, muttering in his sleep
hey boy you balanced boy are you strong now,
poised to recover every coming slip,
& cannot answer yes, or truly know.

The day goes down in one, but even so
he winces like it's someone else's dregs;
life's whizzing by but shit the living's slow,
gone out of love with love & sick of drugs.

Tom sits up late & reads about the sun,
he keeps his lusts stacked crumpled on a shelf
along with other written-out regrets;
and, glancing past his mirror, might have seen
a vast abstraction peering at itself,
like cowardice perhaps, but he forgets.

5. T-Bird

'These dreams of flying & this — o this — vague
feeling from want to want; of you, my dear,
a paralyzing like that helps me dare
a little, little.' Humming the Thunder Rag,
Tom checked his face & fixed his dandy rig
against himself, then slammed & locked the door
on both his loves, expression growing dour,
too thick to take & much too dumb to beg.

His false retelling made harmonic jars
between his stories, tuned his self to be
strung up like lightning from the yawning jaws
& technicolor guts of clouds, 'til he,
sickened by strain & noise & all that jazz,
asked 'why's the dead boy, singing, dressed like me?'

7. The Hint

Tom says 'I'll get me coat,' then tries to stand
& face his crowd, but finds that now it sees
he lives by misdirection, sleight-of-hand
& conjuring in personalities;
flamboyant Gothic, never quite at ease,
twisting beyond its architect's control,
his fond imagining blindly portrays
plans of the human animal, its soul

bound up in title-deeds that someone stole,
not that that changed things much, just made him
                    more
detached, discounted, typecast in his role
of braggart, drunkard, lecher, spendthrift, bore.
What was that masked man? Tom can't say for sure,
except it wasn't anything he'd planned
to end so lost in seeming that he saw
the state he was, & called it fairyland.

Afterword: A Truth Undisguised

Since writing the introduction to this collection, the political climate in the UK has slid still further towards widespread distrust and unfocused fear of the 'Other'. In consequence, it has come to seem worth noting that the writers herein represent four continents as well as myriad differences of belief and individual passions. In such times as these, the unifying humanity expressed and shared through art must, I believe, be both acknowledged and celebrated.

Oz Hardwick,
Leeds, September 2005